Animal Graphs

Pets Graph

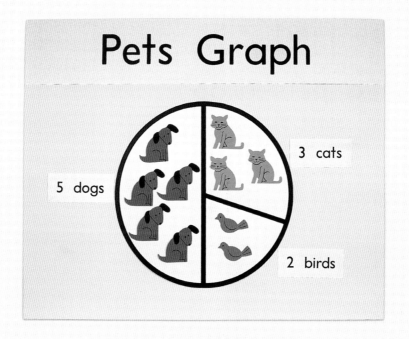

5 dogs

3 cats

2 birds

On Monday,

some of the children

helped the teacher

to make a pets graph.

They made it with pictures

of pets.

Pets Graph

Daniel said to the teacher,
"Three children like cats,
two children like birds,
and five children like dogs."

"Dogs are the favourite pets,"
said Kim.

Pets Graph

5 dogs

3 cats

2 birds

On Tuesday,

Kim said,

"Can we make a zoo graph today?"

"We can put elephants and tigers
and monkeys on a zoo graph,"
said Daniel.

The children helped Kim and Daniel

make the zoo graph.

They made pictures of

three elephants,

one tiger,

and six monkeys.

Kim and Daniel put the pictures

of the elephants,

the tiger,

and the monkeys

on the zoo graph.

Zoo Graph

"I like this graph, too,"
said the teacher.
"I can see three elephants,
one tiger,
and six monkeys."

Zoo Graph

6 monkeys

3 elephants

1 tiger

"Six children like monkeys,"
said Daniel.
"Monkeys are the favourite zoo animals."

Zoo Graph

6 monkeys

3 elephants

1 tiger

Pets Graph

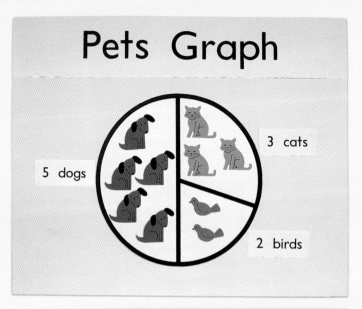

5 dogs

3 cats

2 birds

Zoo Graph

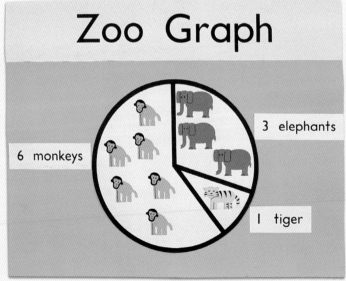

6 monkeys

3 elephants

1 tiger